Keith Roberts

ITALIAN
RENAISSANCE
PAINTING

PHAIDON   E.P. DUTTON
Oxford   New York

FT. WORTH PUBLIC LIBRARY

The author and publishers would like to thank all those museum authorities and private owners who have kindly allowed works in their possession to be reproduced.

759.5
I

Phaidon Press Limited, Littlegate House, St Ebbe's Street, Oxford
Published in the United States of America by E. P. Dutton & Co., Inc.

First published 1976

© 1976 Elsevier Publishing Projects SA, Lausanne/Smeets Illustrated Projects, Weert
Text © 1976 by Keith Roberts

All rights reserved
No part of this publication may be reproduced, stored in a retrieval system, or transmitted in any form or by any means, electronic, mechanical, photocopying, recording or otherwise, without the prior permission of the publishers

ISBN 0 7148 1745 7
Library of Congress Catalog Card Number: 76-1345

Printed in The Netherlands

ITALIAN RENAISSANCE PAINTING

'Hollywood', a wit once remarked, 'is not a place – it's a state of mind.' A distinction of this type is useful when considering the complex and mysterious phenomenon known as the Renaissance. What makes it difficult to analyse is that the Renaissance represents an attitude not only towards art but also towards life itself. It affected the way men thought about religion, politics, literature, society and the past. Handwriting, the design of a chair or a fabric, the decoration on a plate: there was hardly anything outside its sphere of influence. It encouraged experiment and change, it brought about an expansion of possibilities – what the Chinese nowadays might call 'a great leap forward'. In the fifteenth and sixteenth centuries the Renaissance spread from Italy all over Europe.

In Italian painting, the subject of this book, the Renaissance involved many innovations: more observant attitudes to nature led to the development of landscape painting (Plates 9, 15, 16, 19, 27); a growing awareness of individuality encouraged the growth of portraiture (Plates 11, 22, 23, 28, 29); researches into anatomy enabled artists to depict the human body with greater accuracy, variety and grace (Plates 1, 9, 19, 25, 36); the development of perspective allowed painters to set their figures in convincing space (Plates 2, 5, 8, 13, 16, 17, 19, 31); the study of geometry became a key to harmonious pictorial composition (Plates 8, 9, 19, 31, 32); and the cult of pagan Antiquity nourished artistic wisdom and creative inspiration (Plates 1, 15, 17, 19, 26, 30, 31, 35, 47, 48). The word *renaissance* is the French for 're-birth', and at the heart of fifteenth- and sixteenth-century thinking was the creation of a culture that could also be looked upon as a revival of the standards and many of the assumptions of the ancient world of Greece and Rome. It seems a strange philosophy now, in a world of rockets and supermarkets, television and heart transplants, and for all its decorative splendour, beauty and colourful swagger, the Renaissance represents a concept with which it is very difficult to come to terms.

Unlike most twentieth-century developments in art, which have been made outside ordinary social, religious or political contexts, and hence have been subject to many sudden changes of fashion, Renaissance art was created inside the social structure. Italian painters worked for the Church, the city states, ruling families and private clients, and were bound by the conventions of decorum and tradition. There is no record of an artist starving, like Van Gogh, because his work was too *avant-garde*; although a painter may have done less well if he fell too far behind the current style. What gives Renaissance art its enormous and lasting strength is that the far-reaching ideas of genius – and one thinks of Masaccio (Plate 1), Leonardo (Plates 21, 29), Raphael (Plate 31) or Michelangelo (Plate 36) – were often applied to works that expressed profound and universal emotions and were intended to have very wide appeal.

All the pictures in this book illustrate religious and mythological themes or are portraits and allegories. The unparalleled richness of Renaissance painting can partly be explained by the wealth of new ideas being poured into a relatively narrow

ART

1

3

range of creative outlets circumscribed by traditional requirements and expectations. This is especially true of religious art, the largest and most important category of painting, where every subject had its particular rules. It was usual, for example, to show the Virgin Mary in a reddish dress covered by a dark – invariably blue – mantle; and this is how she was painted by Masaccio (Plate 2), Gentile (Plate 4), Fra Angelico (Plate 7), Crivelli (Plate 20), Raphael (Plate 32), Michelangelo (Plate 33) and Parmigianino (Plate 38).

But as long as the basic elements were included in a well-known subject, artists were often free to introduce all manner of further detail. A picture like *The Martyrdom of St. Sebastian* (Plate 19), by the Pollaiuolo brothers, is not only a cult image for the faithful, to remind them of the sacrifices made for Christianity, but also what amounts to a pictorial index of Renaissance interests. The Roman arch symbolizes the cult of Antiquity and the muscular archers the new researches into anatomy. The beautiful view of the Arno valley in the background testifies to a fresh and direct observation of nature, while the way in which the space sweeps back to the horizon suggests a knowledge of the newly developed principles of perspective. *The Martyrdom of St. Sebastian* is a picture that teems with vitality.

Renaissance painting is not only rich but also extremely varied in mood and tone. This variety was encouraged by the political structure of Italy, which was made up of many self-governing city states. Several regions developed individual variants of the current style – rather like dialects – and it is customary to think of Piero della Francesca (Plate 9) as Umbrian, Bellini (Plates 28, 30) and Titian (Plates 44, 47) as Venetian, Tura (Plate 18) as Ferrarese, Mantegna (Plate 17) as North Italian, Moroni (Plate 43) as Brescian, and Masaccio (Plates 1, 2) and Botticelli (Plates 23, 26) as Florentine. At the same time, when city states were constantly vying with one another, an important artist could add to local prestige. This encouraged a cross-fertilization of ideas as painters were lured from one city to another. Leonardo, for example, went from Florence to Milan, and back again, and spent his last years in France; Raphael went from Perugia to Florence, and on to Rome; and Antonello worked in both Naples and Venice.

The Plates

Plate 1. MASACCIO (1401–27/9): *The Expulsion of Adam and Eve from Paradise*. About 1425–27/9. Fresco. Florence, Santa Maria del Carmine (Brancacci Chapel).

This fresco, on the left entrance pier of the Brancacci Chapel (one of the few surviving parts of the original Gothic church of Santa Maria del Carmine), is from a series of frescoes painted by Masaccio, in collaboration with Masolino da Panicale, between 1423 and 1427/9. The series was finally completed by Filippino Lippi in the mid-1480s. The main scenes illustrate episodes from the Life of St. Peter. To a congregation brought up on the flatter, stiffer and more decorative late Gothic idiom of an artist like Lorenzo Monaco, or even Gentile da Fabriano (Plate 4), this image of Adam and Eve must have seemed astonishing in its anatomical and emotional realism. It was these qualities, added to an almost indefinable grandeur, that would have impressed the young Michelangelo when, over sixty years later, he copied Masaccio's figures.

Plate 2. MASACCIO (1401–27/9): *The Virgin and Child Enthroned*. 1426. Panel, 135·5 × 73 cm. (53¼ × 28¾ in.) London, National Gallery.

Although Masaccio is universally recognized as one of the founders of Italian Renaissance painting, very little is known about him. There is only one strictly documented work, an altarpiece of many panels (polyptych), painted for a side chapel in the church of the Carmine at Pisa in 1426. Plate 2 reproduces the central panel.

Plate 3. FRA FILIPPO LIPPI (c.1406–69): *The Virgin and Child*. About 1440–5. Panel, 80 × 51 cm. (31⅝ × 20⅛ in.) Washington, National Gallery of Art (Samuel H. Kress Collection).

Lippi, an orphan, was a novice at the Carmine in Florence and took the Carmelite vows in 1421. Ten years later, when he is first documented as a painter, he was still at the Carmine, where Masaccio had worked in the Brancacci Chapel (see Plate 1), and it is probable that he was a pupil of the older artist. He was certainly influenced by Masaccio's style, as one can see here by comparing the Christ-child in Plate 2 with Lippi's Infant in Plate 3.

Plate 4. GENTILE DA FABRIANO (c.1370–1427): *The Adoration of the Magi*. 1423. Panel, 300 × 282 cm. (120 × 112 in.) Florence, Uffizi.

The elaborate altarpiece of which the main panel is reproduced here is one of the last and richest expressions of the Late Gothic style. In comparison with the Angelico/Lippi interpretation (Plate 7), Gentile's feeling for space is more rudimentary and his knowledge of anatomy less developed. But the weaknesses of his style are all but submerged in the wealth of sharply observed detail, the rich fabrics, varied headgear, splendid horses and other animals. The artist has even found room for two monkeys. Although it is customary to speak of Italian painters belonging to this or that 'school' (Florentine, Sienese, Venetian, etc.), these categories can sometimes be misleading. Gentile da Fabriano, for example, is known to have worked in Venice, Brescia, Florence, Siena and Rome, and his style, which is also found

in the courtly art of France, Burgundy, Germany and Bohemia, is known as 'International Gothic'.

Plate 5. FRA ANGELICO (active 1417; d.1455): *Scenes from the Life of St. Lawrence.* About 1447–9. Fresco. Vatican, Chapel of Nicholas V.

On the left, the Saint is receiving the treasures of the Church from Pope Sixtus II; on the right he distributes alms. It is known that Angelico employed several assistants at the time of the Vatican commission, and that the highest paid was Benozzo Gozzoli (see Plate 6), whose hand has been detected in several of the figures. In the scene on the right, for example, the two women are thought to have been painted by Gozzoli. Lawrence was one of the seven deacons at Rome during the pontificate of Sixtus II and suffered martyrdom in the year 258 during the persecution of the Emperor Valerian.

Plate 6. BENOZZO GOZZOLI (1420–97): *The Journey of the Magi.* About 1459. Fresco. Florence, Medici-Riccardi Palace, Chapel.

Although this festive scene, illustrating the joyful procession of the Magi to Bethlehem, might seem to present no problems of interpretation, and to be as easy to understand now as it was in the fifteenth century, in at least one respect it reveals a profound difference of thinking: the Magi are likenesses of members of the Medici family, for whose Florentine palace the fresco was painted. It is hard to imagine a present-day Maecenas – say, an American millionaire – commissioning a fresco in which he himself appeared as a Biblical character.

Plate 7. FRA ANGELICO (active 1417; d.1455) and FRA FILIPPO LIPPI (*c.*1406–69): *The Adoration of the Magi.* About 1450–5(?). Panel, diameter 137·4 cm. (54 in.) Washington, National Gallery of Art (Samuel H. Kress Collection).

The authorship of this *tondo* (circular work), which is among the most enchanting of fifteenth-century Italian pictures, is not absolutely certain; but it seems probable that the design and some of the figures (notably the Virgin and Child) are by Fra Angelico, the painting being completed after his death by Filippo Lippi. Some of the details, which to modern eyes are simply pleasurable, have a symbolic significance, which would have been apparent to fifteenth-century spectators. The peacock, for example, was regarded as a symbol of immortality.

Plate 8. DOMENICO VENEZIANO (active 1438; d.1461): *The Virgin and Child with Saints* (the 'St. Lucy Altarpiece'). About 1445. Panel, 209 × 213 cm. (83 × 85 in.) Florence, Uffizi.

An early example of what was to become a very popular type of devotional picture, the *sacra conversazione* (Italian for 'sacred conversation'), in which the Virgin and Child are shown in a timeless setting with attendant saints grouped on either side. It was a more sophisticated, and more intimate, version of the older type of altarpiece (which was still produced) with saints shown isolated in separate spaces and often on different panels. Domenico's main preoccupation as an artist (which he passed on to his assistant, Piero della Francesca, see Plate 9) was the creation of serenely idealized religious imagery by means of simplified detail, the construction of harmonious space with the help of architectural elements based on Classical motifs, and the careful observation of colours as they are modified by the fall of light. The Saints are Francis, John the Baptist, Zenobius and Lucy. John's gesture ('Behold the Lamb of God') invites the beholder to pray.

6

Plate 9.   PIERO DELLA FRANCESCA (active 1439; d.1492): *The Baptism of Christ.* About 1450–5(?). Panel, 167 × 116 cm. (66 × 45¾ in.) London, National Gallery.

The subject chosen for the main altarpiece of a Catholic church was usually related to the Saint or Holy Person who was the Patron of that church. This picture was painted for the high altar of the Church of St. John the Baptist at Sansepolcro, a small Tuscan town, which is depicted in the background. The use of real locations in the backgrounds of religious scenes was in no way frivolous, but was part of the underlying strategy of Renaissance artists and ecclesiastical patrons to make the Bible stories as clear and vivid as possible. Preachers, indeed, often exhorted their congregations to imagine Biblical events in contemporary settings. The figure of Christ is an early example of another Renaissance tenet: that spiritual perfection could be reflected in the harmonious beauty of the human body, a doctrine that reached its highest expression in Michelangelo's Adam (see Plate 36).

Plate 10.   ALESSO BALDOVINETTI (*c.*1426–99): *Portrait of a Lady in Yellow.* About 1465. Panel, 62·9 × 40·6 cm. (24¾ × 16 in.) London, National Gallery.

This type of profile portrait was influenced by the Renaissance enthusiasm for Classical coins and cameos, and by contemporary medals (those of Pisanello, for example). Like so many artists of his day, Baldovinetti did not confine himself to painting; he also designed mosaics, stained-glass windows and *intarsie.* This is the only portrait that is securely attributable to him.

Plate 11.   DOMENICO GHIRLANDAIO (1449–94): *Portrait of Giovanna Tornabuoni.* 1488. Panel, 77 × 49 cm. (30⅜ × 19⅜ in.) Lugano, Thyssen Collection.

This portrait, which develops the plain profile image of Baldovinetti by the introduction of background accessories, represents Giovanna degli Albizzi (1468–88?), who married (in June, 1486) Lorenzo Tornabuoni, a member of one of the leading Florentine families. Lorenzo's father, Giovanni, had commissioned Ghirlandaio to paint a series of frescoes in the choir of S. Maria Novella, Florence, and in one of the scenes, Giovanna is shown in the same pose, though at full length. It is probable that this reduced version was painted shortly afterwards. Giovanna died in childbirth, possibly in 1488, and it may be that both portraits were posthumous. The Latin inscription on the paper can be translated: 'Oh Art, if you could express her manners and her mind, there would then be no lovelier picture upon earth.'

Plate 12.   SASSETTA (1392?–1450): *St. Francis renounces his Earthly Father.* 1437–44. Panel, 87·6 × 52·1 cm. (34½ × 20¾ in.) London, National Gallery.

One of a series of panels, illustrating the life of St. Francis, from an altarpiece painted for the high altar of the church of S.Francesco at Sansepolcro. Six further scenes are in the National Gallery, and a recent restoration has recovered Sassetta's gay colours and rich gilding. Like Masaccio (Plate 2), Sassetta combines a use of the new perspective with the flat, gilded background of the older style. Francis of Assisi (1181/2–1226) was disowned by his father, a rich cloth merchant, when he gave away all he owned and devoted himself to helping the poor. He founded the very influential Franciscan Order. While this very altarpiece was being completed, Pope Eugenius IV provided the Order with a separate Vicar General (1443).

Plate 13.   ANTONELLO DA MESSINA (active 1456; d.1479): *St. Jerome in his Study.* About 1460. Panel, 45·7 × 36·2 cm. (18 × 14¼ in.) London, National Gallery.

Many – perhaps most – fifteenth-century Italian painters were accustomed to working

on large-scale frescoes and altarpieces. Minute detail was generally outside their range of sympathies. However, when portraits and religious paintings by Flemish masters like Jan van Eyck, Hugo van der Goes and Memlinc began to appear in Italian collections, their meticulous technique and attention to the smallest visual incident was greatly admired, and proved influential. Antonello da Messina was the Italian artist who benefited most from the Northern example. With its vistas, elaborately patterned floor, complicated still-life and careful delineation of the fall of light, *St. Jerome* is very Eyckian in feeling. Indeed, a traveller who saw it in 1529 was not sure whether it was by Antonello, Van Eyck or Memlinc. Like the Flemings, Antonello also learned how to paint in an elaborate oil technique, which he passed on to Venetian painters like Giovanni Bellini (see Plate 28). See also Plate 22.

Plate 14. PAOLO UCCELLO (*c*.1397–1475): *St. George and the Dragon*. About 1460.
Canvas, 56·5 × 74·3 cm. (22¼ × 29¼ in.) London, National Gallery.
Uccello was fascinated by perspective, but he approached it less as a science than as a kind of game. St. George on his white horse is like a mechanical model that you wind up. But the picture has enormous charm. Two episodes in the story are combined in the single scene: the Princess holds the dragon on a leash, but this only happened *after* it was vanquished by St. George. The disturbance in the sky is probably meant to suggest heavenly intervention – as it is in Tintoretto's version (Plate 45) – though God the Father is not shown. It is rare for paintings on canvas to survive from the mid-fifteenth century.

Plate 15. PIERO DI COSIMO (1461/2–1521): *A Forest Fire*. About 1505–7(?). Panel, 71 × 203 cm. (28¼ × 81 in.) Oxford, Ashmolean Museum.
One of a series of pictures intended to decorate a room. Although the enchanting panel might seem to be self-explanatory and not in need of a recondite interpretation, the whole series probably illustrated a story or 'programme'. Panofsky made the ingenious suggestion that the series symbolizes the growth of civilization through the control of fire, and that the Ashmolean picture represents the Age before Vulcan, 'when man's knowledge was primitive and forest fires raged unchecked'.

Plate 16. GIOVANNI BELLINI (active *c*.1459; d.1516): *The Agony in the Garden*. About 1465. Panel, 81·3 × 127 cm. (32 × 50 in.) London, National Gallery.
The most important of Bellini's surviving early works. As with the version by his brother-in-law, Mantegna (Plate 17), the design goes back to a drawing by his father, Jacopo Bellini. In both paintings the sleeping disciples provided the artists with the opportunity to experiment with perspective. But the most haunting feature of Bellini's panel is the dawn light, rendered with a virtuosity remarkable for the mid-1460s.

Plate 17. ANDREA MANTEGNA (*c*.1430–1506): *The Agony in the Garden*. About 1460–70. Panel, 63 × 80 cm. (24¾ × 31½ in.) London, National Gallery.
The walled city in the background is meant to be Jerusalem; Judas and the soldiers are approaching along the road. Although many of the ingredients are similar, the effect of Mantegna's painting is very different from Bellini's version. Mantegna was less interested in atmosphere and the play of light; his interpretation is harder and more linear. As the reconstruction of Jerusalem suggests, he was also much more interested in the Classical past. At the same time, he was quite capable of inserting wildlife into the scene: look at the rabbits and at the birds in the stream and on the tree.

8

Plate 18. COSIMO TURA (*c*.1430–95): *The Virgin and Child Enthroned*. About 1480.
Panel, 239 × 102 cm. (94¼ × 40 in.) London, National Gallery.

A characteristic example of the mannered, knotty style of Tura, who worked much
at Ferrara, for the Este Court. He was influenced by the young Mantegna (compare,
for example, the sharply outlined forms in Plate 17). The throne is decorated with
two tablets, on which are some of the words of the Ten Commandments in Hebrew.

Plate 19. ANTONIO (*c*.1432–98) and PIERO DEL POLLAIUOLO (*c*.1441–96): *The Martyrdom of St. Sebastian*. ?1475. Panel, 291·5 × 202·6 cm. (114¾ × 79¼
in.) London, National Gallery.

Painted for the Oratory of St. Sebastian attached to the Church of the SS.Annunziata
at Florence. The Pollaiuoli were brothers and ran a flourishing workshop in Florence
typical of the period in its range of activities: both were sculptors as well as painters,
and Antonio at least was also a goldsmith. The landscape background is a *tour
de force* for the date, and the archers show the painters' newly acquired skill in
rendering complicated poses in convincing perspective.

Plate 20. CARLO CRIVELLI (active 1457; d.1493): *The Annunciation, with St. Emidius*.
1486. Panel transferred to canvas, 207 × 146·5 cm. (81½ × 57¾ in.)
London, National Gallery.

A very good example of the way in which a universal subject – the Annunciation
of the Virgin Birth to Mary by the Angel Gabriel – has been modified by the
demands of a particular situation. The picture was painted for the Church of the
Annunciation at Ascoli Piceno (the artist's home town in later life), to celebrate
certain rights of self-government granted to the town by Pope Sixtus IV in 1482.
By 1486, when Crivelli painted the work, Sixtus was dead, and it is the arms
of his successor, Innocent VIII, that appear along the base. An attendant Saint
is not usually included in an Annunciation, but St. Emidius was the Patron of
Ascoli Piceno (a model of which he actually carries in his left hand), so he has
been placed rather prominently next to Gabriel. The architecture, enlivened at
the left with spectators, and the still-life objects both inside and above the Virgin's
chamber, show particularly well the way in which a religious subject could be
treated in wholly contemporary visual terms.

Plate 21. LEONARDO DA VINCI (1452–1519): '*The Virgin of the Rocks*.' About 1480.
Panel, transferred to canvas, 197 × 119·5 cm. (79 × 43¾ in.) Paris,
Louvre.

The greatest of Leonardo's early works, probably painted in Florence just before
he moved to Milan in or about 1482, and one of the most beautiful pictorial
inventions in European painting. The Christ-child, supported by an angel, is blessing
the infant Baptist. The scene takes place in a rocky grotto at sunset. What makes
the picture so miraculous is the way in which acute observation of the real world,
evident in the flowers and plants, the structure of the rocks and the details of
anatomy, is subtly transformed by the equally rigorous claims of imagination. *The
Virgin of the Rocks* is both naturalistic and visionary, extraordinarily concrete – no
one before Leonardo had described so accurately the soft, plump flesh and fine-spun
hair of babies, or noticed the taut fold of flesh between the thumb and index
finger (of the Virgin's hand) – and yet hauntingly mysterious. A later, more prosaic
but better preserved version, partly by pupils but certainly worked on by Leonardo
himself, is in the National Gallery, London.

Plate 22. ANTONELLO DA MESSINA (active 1456; d.1479): *Portrait of a man*. About 1475. Panel, 35·6 × 25·5 cm. (14 × 10 in.) London, National Gallery. The meticulous technique is heavily influenced by Flemish portraits (see Note to Plate 13). The comparison with the Botticelli portrait is instructive (see Note to Plate 23).

Plate 23. BOTTICELLI (*c*.1445–1510): *Portrait of a Young Man*. About 1480. Panel, 37·5 × 28·3 cm. (14¾ × 11⅛ in.) London, National Gallery.

A type of portrait, with the figure cut at the chest, and with a plain background, that became very popular in the 1470s and 1480s. Botticelli's style, in comparison with Antonello's (Plate 22), is more linear (look at the simplified drawing of the eyes) and less detailed. Antonello paints in the eyelashes, seemingly every hair that escapes from under the red cap, and the stubble on the face.

Plate 24. ANDREA DEL CASTAGNO (*c*.1420–57): *The Young David*. About 1450. Leather, 115·6 × 76·9 × 41 cm. (45½ × 30¼ × 16⅛ in.) Washington, National Gallery of Art (Widener Collection).

Castagno was an important mid-century Florentine painter who developed a vivid, dynamic style influenced by the art of Masaccio and the sculptor, Donatello. Much of his work has been destroyed, including the frescoes in the church of S. Egidio, Florence, where he painted alongside Domenico Veneziano (Plate 8) and Piero della Francesca (Plate 9). *The Young David* was probably used as a tournament shield and is a rare survivor of a wide range of ephemeral work that occupied even the most celebrated artists in the fifteenth and sixteenth centuries.

Plate 25. Detail of Plate 26.

Plate 26. BOTTICELLI (*c*. 1445–1510): *The Birth of Venus*. About 1490. Canvas, 175 × 278 cm. (70 × 111 in.) Florence, Uffizi.

Venus, Classical goddess of Love, rides on a shell, which is being blown towards the shore by two Zephyrs symbolizing the winds. Possibly painted for Lorenzo di Pierfrancesco de' Medici, and probably intended to have elaborate, Neoplatonic, quasi-Christian philosophic overtones, which a lack of precise documents makes it very difficult to reconstruct with any precision. The composition was based on formulae normally reserved for the Baptism of Christ, but the pose of Venus – like that of Masaccio's Eve (Plate 1) – derives from a celebrated Antique statue. *The Birth of Venus* may well have been intended as a tribute to Antique painting: Apelles had painted a *Birth of Venus*, described by Pliny, an author well known to Botticelli and the Medicean circle of intellectuals.

Plate 27. Ascribed to GIORGIONE (*c*.1478–1510), but perhaps finished by TITIAN: *Fête Champêtre*. About 1510. Canvas, 110 × 138 cm. (44 × 55 in.) Paris, Louvre.

Although the authorship of this picture is far from certain – it may have been begun by Giorgione and finished by him, or begun by him and completed by Titian – no other work sums up so well the Giorgionesque spirit. The mood is pastoral and sensual; man is at peace with nature and with himself. The sound of gentle music adds to the contentment. The landscape is no longer just a background for the figures; they are actually *in* the landscape. The painting has a subject as well as a mood, however, but this too is as puzzling as the authorship. It may well go back to a classical source. Giorgione's conception of art was one of the major influences on Titian, and the female nude in natural surroundings a perennial theme, as seen in *Diana and Actaeon*, painted almost fifty years later (Plate 47).

Plate 28. GIOVANNI BELLINI (active *c.*1459; d.1516): *The Doge Leonardo Loredan.* About 1501–5. Panel, 61·5 × 45 cm. (24¼ × 17¾ in.) London, National Gallery.

The finest of Bellini's portraits, and among the best preserved of his works, this picture represents Leonardo Loredan (1436–1521), who became the Doge of Venice in 1501. Although the treatment of the rich fabric is masterly, it does not detract from the face and, in particular, from the expression of wisdom tinged with sympathy and understanding. The way the figure is cut off at chest level creates the impression of a portrait bust. The next step in the development of portraiture, already taken in Florence, was the inclusion of the hands and arms. The '*Mona Lisa*' (Plate 29), dating from only three or four years later, is a masterly solution of the problem.

Plate 29. LEONARDO DA VINCI (1452–1519): *Portrait of an Unknown Woman ('Mona Lisa')*. About 1506–8. Panel, 76·8 × 53 cm. (30¼ × 21 in.) Paris, Louvre.

Although this is the most famous picture in the world, very little is actually known about it. Even the date when it was painted is uncertain. It is not a portrait in the modern sense, or even in the sense that Antonello da Messina (Plate 22) or Bellini (Plate 28) would have understood the term. The smiling expression, which has so haunted subsequent generations, has much more in common with Leonardo's idealized heads (such as that of the angel in Plate 21) than with any likely sitter. The first question that everyone sooner or later asks – 'what is she thinking? why is she smiling?' – is almost certainly irrelevant. What Leonardo wanted to do was to suggest the *idea* of the human personality and the workings of the mind by an image that suggested mystery. The woman is actually seated in an armchair by a window – the picture was cut at the sides, at an unknown date, and only the bases of the window frame are now visible. Like the background in *The Virgin of the Rocks* (Plate 21), the rocky landscape in the background reveals Leonardo's obsession with the natural world, which he came to feel was both mysterious and threatening. In the landscape, as in the face, Leonardo's technique was to re-arrange scrupulously observed naturalistic detail so as to create an idealized effect.

Plate 30. GIOVANNI BELLINI (active *c.*1459–1516): *The Feast of the Gods.* 1514. Canvas, 170 × 188 cm. (67 × 74 in.) Washington, National Gallery of Art (Widener Collection).

Painted for Alfonso d'Este as part of the decoration of the Alabaster Room in the Castle of Ferrara. When Titian, a few years later, came to paint three companion pieces (which included the *Bacchus and Ariadne* in the National Gallery in London), he 'modernized' Bellini's picture by repainting the background in a more dynamic style. X-rays have proved that the gods and goddesses, who have gathered for the Feast of Bacchus, were originally grouped in front of a curtain of trees, of which a part remains on the right. The subject was taken from Ovid, who was extremely popular in the Renaissance (see Titian's *Diana and Actaeon*, Plate 47).

Plate 31. RAPHAEL (1483–1520): '*The School of Athens.*' About 1509–11. Fresco. Rome, Vatican, Stanza della Segnatura.

One of the frescoes in the Stanza della Segnatura, the first of the apartments in the Vatican that Raphael and his assistants painted for Pope Julius II and his successor, Leo X. The first room was painted between the end of 1508 and 1511 and has as its theme the operation of the Intellect, symbolized by the four faculties, Theology, Philosophy, Jurisprudence and Poetry. '*The School of Athens*' (the title, incidentally, seems to date only from the late seventeenth century) is devoted to

Philosophy. At the centre of the composition are the figures of Plato and Aristotle. The noble building can be related to the work of the contemporary architect, Bramante. Raphael himself was also active as an architect and in 1514 succeeded Bramante as Chief Architect of Saint Peter's, a post later held by Michelangelo.

Plate 32. RAPHAEL (1483–1520): *The Virgin and Child with St. John the Baptist and St. Nicholas of Bari ('The Ansidei Madonna')*. 1505? Panel, 209·6 × 148·6 cm. (82½ × 58½ in.) London, National Gallery.

A fine and very well preserved example of Raphael's religious imagery, in which, following the tradition of Domenico Veneziano (Plate 8), Piero (Plate 9) and Leonardo (Plate 21), the harmony and balance of the composition and the refined delicacy of the Virgin and the Child come to symbolize an exalted spiritual state. The altarpiece was painted for the Ansidei family chapel in the church of S. Fiorenzo at Perugia. The chapel was under the protection of St. Nicholas of Bari, which explains his presence on the right, together with one of his attributes, the three bags of gold, representing the dowry he is said to have given to three maidens to save them from degradation. Readers who turn to Piero's *Baptism* (Plate 9) will notice an interesting difference: in scenes from the New Testament the Baptist is shown (in keeping with the Biblical text) as more or less the same age as Christ, and this is implicit in Leonardo's *Virgin of the Rocks* (Plate 21) and in Michelangelo's *tondo* (Plate 33), where both are babes; but Raphael follows the tradition usual in non-narrative devotional paintings also to be found in the Domenico Veneziano (Plate 8) of a fully-grown Baptist in attendance on the still infant Christ.

Plate 33. MICHELANGELO (1475–1564): *The Holy Family ('The Doni Tondo')*. About 1504. Panel, diameter 120 cm. (48 in.) Florence, Uffizi.

This is the only easel picture known that is certainly from the hand of Michelangelo. It was commissioned by a Florentine, Angelo Doni – perhaps to celebrate his marriage – but apparently there was a long wrangle over the fee. The compactness of the group, which looks as if it were carved out of a piece of marble, reveals the influence of Michelangelo's activities as a sculptor. The figures in the background attest to his life-long obsession with the male nude; but they would not have been included in a devotional work of this kind merely for pleasure. It has been shrewdly suggested that they symbolize the Pagan Life, which was superseded by the Era of Grace, personified by Christ.

Plate 34. Ascribed to GIORGIONE (*c*.1478–1510): *The Virgin and Child with St. Anthony of Padua and St. Roch*. About 1508. Canvas, 92 × 133 cm. (36¾ × 53¾ in.) Madrid, Prado.

A Venetian equivalent to Raphael's *Ansidei Madonna* (Plate 32), this beautiful picture was almost certainly painted by one of the most mysterious of Renaissance masters, Giorgione. Giorgione, who can be regarded as something of a transitional figure between Giovanni Bellini and Titian, introduced into Venetian art a new softness, tinged on occasion with mystery, and a greater sense of mood and atmosphere. Both the attendant saints had local associations. St. Anthony (1195–1231) was the Patron Saint of nearby Padua, where his relics were venerated. St. Roch (on the right), who died in 1327, was the Saint invoked against plague, always a particular risk in the humid climate of Venice, where indeed he was especially venerated and where, after 1485, his relics were kept. Both Giorgione (certainly) and Titian (probably) died of the plague.

Plate 35. LORENZO LOTTO (*c.*1480–1556): *Portrait of Andrea Odoni.* 1527. Canvas, 101·5 × 114 cm. (40 × 45½ in.) Hampton Court, Royal Collection (reproduced by gracious permission of Her Majesty the Queen).

One of those rare instances when a work of Renaissance art is documented fairly soon after it was painted, this picture was described in 1532: 'the half-length portrait in oil of this Messer Andrea, contemplating antique marble fragments, is by the hand of Lorenzo Lotto.' And we know that it hung in Odoni's bedroom, together with furniture painted by a pupil of Titian. Odoni collected Roman antiquities, and his portrait is a perfect symbol of the Renaissance obsession with the Classical past.

Plate 36. MICHELANGELO (1475–1564): *The Creation of Adam.* 1511–12. Fresco. Rome, Vatican, Sistine Chapel.

The best known scene from the vast fresco cycle with which Michelangelo covered the ceiling of the Sistine Chapel, at the command of Pope Julius II. The chapel itself measures approximately 44 by 132 feet. Like Giotto and Masaccio (Plate 1) before him, Michelangelo was not interested in elaborate, detailed settings for his figures. He relied on the expressive qualities of the human figure to convey the full meaning. He also had a highly professional knowledge of what was involved in painting scenes and figures that would be seen from some sixty feet below. Thus, in the preparatory drawing for the Adam, the outline is more detailed and the muscle structure more defined than in the final painting, where the forms have been generalized. Adam's pose was partly influenced by Classical statues of reclining River Gods. The male nudes above and below the main scene, and at right angles to it, are four of the twenty-four figures of athletes, whose purpose was to link, visually and dramatically, the Prophets on the sides and ends of the vaulted ceiling with the narrative scenes along the centre.

Plate 37. PONTORMO (1494–1557): *Joseph in Egypt.* About 1515. Panel, 96·5 × 109·5 cm. (38 × 43⅛ in.) London, National Gallery.

An interesting example of the way in which even a relatively small commission could be farmed out among a number of artists. This panel is one of a series, illustrating the life of Joseph, painted by Andrea del Sarto, Pontormo, Granacci, and Bacchiacca, for a Florentine patron.

Plate 38. PARMIGIANINO (1503–40): *The Mystic Marriage of St. Catherine.* About 1530. Panel, 74·2 × 57 cm. (29¼ × 22½ in.) London, National Gallery.

The air of conscious elegance; the elongated figure types; the ambiguous space; the suggestion of obscurity (who are the figures in the background?); the asymmetry of the composition (with the bearded man, lower left, arbitrarily relegated to a corner of the design); and the refinement of the execution (look at the treatment of St. Catherine's coiffure): all these elements are characteristic, not only of Parmigianino's art in particular, but also of Mannerism in general. St. Catherine of Alexandria was widely venerated in the Middle Ages and well into the seventeenth century, and often appears in religious pictures, but very little is reliably known about her. Traditionally, she is said to have been a noble lady of Alexandria in the early fourth century who protested against the persecution of Christians by the Emperor Maxentius and was condemned to be tortured on a spiked wheel (the attribute with which she is invariably shown, and which has survived in the Catherine-wheels of our fireworks). The wheel was shattered by her touch, and she had to be beheaded. Another aspect of the legend is that the virginal Catherine,

having refused many suitors, was taken to heaven in a vision and betrothed to Christ by the Virgin Mary. This is the subject of Parmigianino's painting.

Plate 39. CORREGGIO (active 1514; d.1534): *Jupiter and Io*. About 1530. Canvas, 163·5 × 74 cm. (65¼ × 29½ in.) Vienna, Kunsthistorisches Museum. Correggio is famed for the softness and delicacy of his painting and for his command of languorous expression. All these qualities are evident in this picture of Io being seduced by the god, Jupiter, disguised as a cloud.

Plate 40. ROSSO FIORENTINO (1494–1540): *Moses and the Daughters of Jethro*. About 1520. Canvas, 160 × 117 cm. (64 × 46¾ in.) Florence, Uffizi. Rosso was one of the leading figures in the first phase of Italian Mannerism. He worked in Florence and Rome, in Venice (where he became a friend of the writer, Pietro Aretino), and in France, where he went at the invitation of King Francis I to decorate the Grande Galerie at Fontainebleau. The paintings and complicated stucco decoration that he produced were a major influence on the development of Mannerism in France. The heroic nudes in the present picture reveal the influence of Michelangelo, though the way in which the lower figures are arranged more for their decorative than their dramatic effect runs counter to Michelangelo's thinking. The Old Testament subject (Exodus ii,16–17) is here taken as the occasion for a display of brilliant virtuosity.

Plate 41. BRONZINO (1503–72): *An Allegory*. About 1545/6. Panel, 146 × 116 cm. (57½ × 45¾ in.) London, National Gallery. Bronzino was Court Painter to Cosimo I de'Medici, the first Grand Duke of Tuscany, and is best known for his elegant and coldly stylized portraits of members of the Medici family and the court circle. This is the most famous, and probably the finest, of his subject pictures. It is an allegory – a genre of which the Renaissance was very fond – but its precise meaning is no longer clear. The central female figure is undoubtedly Venus and the boy who embraces her is Cupid. The old man in the background has an hour-glass behind him and must be Father Time. The child on the right with roses could be Folly while the girl behind him with the hind-quarters of an animal and with a sting in her tail could be Deceit. The figure tearing her hair on the left may well represent Jealousy. The general meaning of the picture might be that Time reveals sensual pleasure as leading to jealousy and despair. Bronzino was much influenced by the art of Michelangelo, and the pose of Venus and the bald head of Time were possibly derived from the *Doni Tondo* (Plate 33).

Plate 42. DOMENICO PULIGO (1492–1527): *Portrait of a Young Nobleman*. About 1520–5. Panel, 114·2 × 83·5 cm. (45 × 33 in.) England, Private Collection. A charming example of early Mannerist portraiture (look at the cunning use of the red gown to suggest an elongated body and at the long, refined fingers), somewhat influenced by Andrea del Sarto (1486–1530), to whom it was once attributed.

Plate 43. GIOVANNI BATTISTA MORONI (active 1546–7; d.1578): *Portrait of a Man ('The Tailor')*. About 1570. Canvas, 97·8 × 74·9 cm. (38½ × 29½ in.) London, National Gallery. Although he painted religious pictures, which are still to be found in Brescian churches, Moroni is best known for his portraits. This is the most famous of them. Whoever the sitter may be, he was no humble artisan: his suit is one that was the fashion of the middle class.

Plate 44. TITIAN (*c*.1485/90–1576): *Pope Paul III and his Grandsons*. 1546. Canvas, 200 × 173 cm. (80 × 69¼ in.) Naples, Galleria Nazionale di Capodimonte.

This unfinished portrait, painted in Rome in 1546, shows Pope Paul III (1468–1549) together with his two grandsons, Cardinal Alessandro Farnese (1520–89) on the left and Ottavio Farnese (1524–86) on the right. The fact that a man who had enjoyed a liaison of some duration, and had fathered four children, was eligible for the Papacy reveals a good deal about one side of religious life in the sixteenth century. It has often been suggested that the composition of this group portrait, with Ottavio bending forward in a seemingly obsequious manner, reflects a power struggle within the Farnese family. But this is inherently improbable. No one – not even Titian – would have had the audacity or, perhaps, even thought of painting such a picture. The more likely explanation for the admittedly unusual composition is that Paul III was famous for his soft-speaking voice and that his grandson is bending forward to hear what the old man is about to say. The pontificate of Paul III (1534–49) marked a turning point in the history of the Roman Catholic Church. To strengthen Catholicism, in the face of the Reformation, the Turkish threat and the power struggle between Francis I and Charles V for the domination of Europe, Paul approved the introduction of the Inquisition into Italy (1542) and the formation of the Society of Jesus (1540). Above all, he convened the Council of Trent (1545).

Plate 45. JACOPO TINTORETTO (1518–94): *St. George and the Dragon*. About 1560–70. Canvas, 157·5 × 100·3 cm. (62 × 39½ in.) London, National Gallery.

St. George was a Roman convert to Christianity who was tortured and put to death in 303. The legend of his fight with the dragon can be traced back no further than the sixth century. George was made the Patron Saint of England during the reign of Edward III (1327–77). In Tintoretto's picture, a relatively small and very carefully painted work no doubt intended for a private client, St. George kills the dragon while the Princess falls to her knees in flight. In the sky God the Father looks down on the scene.

Plate 46. JACOPO TINTORETTO (1518–94): *Susanna and the Elders*. About 1570. Canvas, 146·6 × 193·6 cm. (58½ × 77½ in.) Vienna, Kunsthistorisches Museum.

The subject is taken from the Book of Daniel, chapter xiii. This is a characteristic example of the Renaissance female nude, which to modern eyes often seems almost grotesquely heavy. The preference for generously endowed girls must have reflected sexual tastes, which in turn would have been influenced by social conditions – the sixteenth century was after all an age in which the modern principles of balanced diet were unknown. In art there was the additional power of aesthetic taste. Tintoretto's Susanna is not only heavy, she is also muscular, and this type of body reveals the influence of Michelangelo, whose style dominated Italian painting in the second half of the sixteenth century. The combination of a large body and a small, graceful head was also typical of Mannerism, a contemporary idiom that had itself absorbed a good deal from Michelangelo. But it also prized ideals on which Michelangelo himself would have frowned: grace, elegance, sophistication, preciosity.

Plate 47. TITIAN (*c*.1485/90–1576): *Diana and her Nymphs surprised by Actaeon*. About 1556–9. Canvas, 188 × 203 cm. (74 × 80 in.) Edinburgh, National Gallery of Scotland (on loan from the Duke of Sutherland).

Among Titian's greatest works, this is one of seven mythological scenes painted

for King Philip II of Spain in the 1550s and early 1560s. It illustrates an episode from Ovid's *Metamorphoses*: one day, while hunting in the forest, Actaeon came across the goddess Diana and her attendant nymphs bathing in a grotto. Diana was furious that her charms should be seen by a mere mortal and she transformed Actaeon into a stag, whereupon he was torn to pieces by his own hounds – the subject of a more sombre canvas now in the National Gallery, London. The variety of poses and the way in which the figures have been arranged in a group that recedes into the space already anticipates the developments of seventeenth-century Baroque design. Some of the poses may have been influenced by Antique sculpture – compare, for example, the crouching nymph (fourth from the right) with the statuette in Lotto's portrait (Plate 35).

Plate 48. PAOLO VERONESE (1528?–88): *Mars and Venus United by Love.* About 1570–80. Canvas, 205·7 × 161 cm. (81 × 63⅜ in.) New York, Metropolitan Museum of Art (Kennedy Fund, 1910).

Like so many Renaissance works of art, this picture has a subject that is not precisely documented. The usual title does not explain, for example, the gesture of the hand at the breast. An alternative suggestion is that the female figure symbolizes Chastity Transformed by Love into Charity. The horse, held back by the Cupid, would then be a symbol of Passion Restrained. The imagery is full of Classical overtones, such as the ruins of an ancient building in the background and the dress of the male figure, a sixteenth-century adaptation of Roman costume.

1. Masaccio (1401–27/9): *The Expulsion of Adam and Eve from Paradise*. About 1425–27/9. Fresco. Florence, Santa Maria del Carmine (Brancacci Chapel)

2. Masaccio (1401–27/9): *The Virgin and Child Enthroned*. 1426. Panel,
135·5 × 73 cm. London, National Gallery

3. Fra Filippo Lippi (*c.*1406–69): *The Virgin and Child*. About 1440–5. Panel,
80 × 51 cm. Washington, National Gallery of Art (Samuel H. Kress Collection)

FORT WORTH PUBLIC LIBRARY

4. Gentile da Fabriano (c.1370–1427): *The Adoration of the Magi*. 1423. Panel, 300 × 282 cm. Florence, Uffizi

5. Fra Angelico (active 1417; d. 1455): *Scenes from the Life of St. Lawrence*. About 1447–9. Fresco. Vatican, Chapel of Pope Nicholas V

6. Benozzo Gozzoli (1420—97): *The Journey of the Magi*. About 1459. Fresco. Florence, Medici-Riccardi

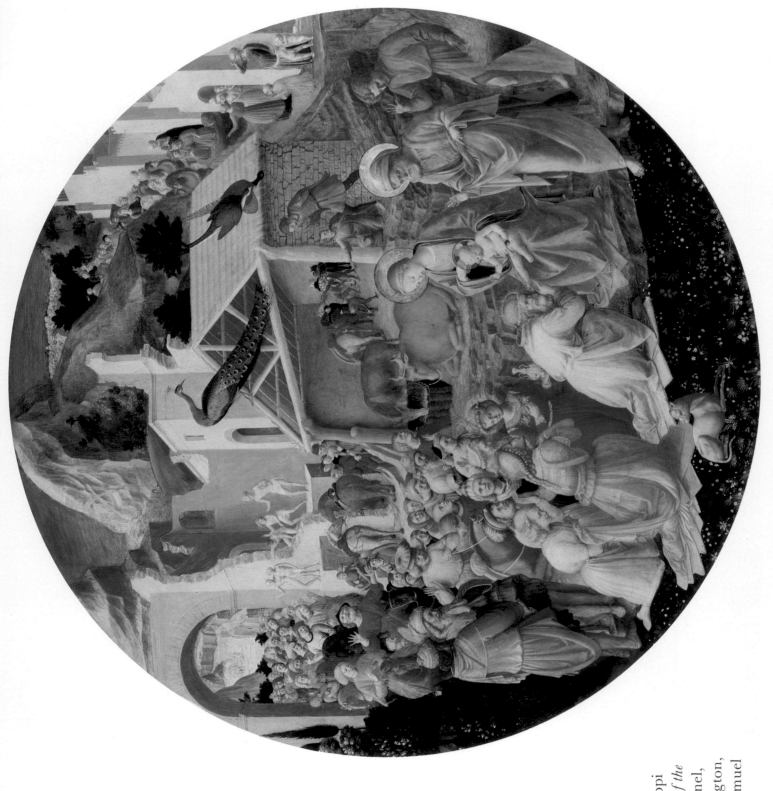

7. Fra Angelico (active 1417;
d. 1455) and Fra Filippo Lippi
(c. 1406–69) : *The Adoration of the
Magi.* About 1450–5 (?). Panel,
diameter 137·4 cm. Washington,
National Gallery of Art (Samuel
H. Kress Collection)

8. Domenico Veneziano (active 1438; d.1461): *The Virgin and Child with Saints (the 'St. Lucy Altarpiece')*.
About 1445. Panel, 209 × 213 cm. Florence, Uffizi

9. Piero della Francesca (active 1439; d. 1492): *The Baptism of Christ*. About 1450–5(?). Panel, 167 × 116 cm. London, National Gallery

10. Alesso Baldovinetti (*c*.1426–99): *Portrait of a Lady in Yellow*. About 1465. Panel, 62·9 × 40·6 cm. London, National Gallery

11. Domenico Ghirlandaio (1449–94): *Portrait of Giovanna Tornabuoni*. 1488. Panel,
77 × 49 cm. Lugano, Thyssen Collection

12. Sassetta (1392?–1450): *St. Francis renounces his Earthly Father*. 1437–44. Panel,
87·6 × 52·1 cm. London, National Gallery

13. Antonello da Messina (active 1456; d. 1479): *St. Jerome in his Study*. About 1460. Panel, 45·7 × 36·2 cm. London, National Gallery

FORT WORTH PUBLIC LIBRARY

14. Paolo Uccello (c.1397–1475): *St. George and the Dragon*. About 1460. Canvas, 56·5 × 74·3 cm. London, National Gallery

15. Piero di Cosimo (1461/2–1521): *A Forest Fire*. About 1505–7(?). Panel, 71 × 203 cm. Oxford, Ashmolean Museum

16. Giovanni Bellini (active *c.*1459; d.1516): *The Agony in the Garden.* About 1465. Panel, 81·3 × 127 cm. London, National Gallery

17 Andrea Mantegna (*c.*1430–1506) : *The Agony in the Garden. About* 1460–70. Panel, 63 × 80 cm. London, National Gallery

18. Cosimo Tura (*c.*1430–95): *The Virgin and Child Enthroned*.
About 1480. Panel, 239 × 102 cm. London, National
Gallery

19. Antonio (*c*.1432–98) and Piero del Pollaiuolo (*c*.1441–96): *The Martyrdom of St. Sebastian.* ?1475.
Panel, 291·5 × 202·6 cm. London, National Gallery

FORT WORTH PUBLIC LIBRARY

20. Carlo Crivelli (active 1457; d.1493): *The Annunciation, with St. Emidius*. 1486. Panel transferred to canvas, 207 × 146·5 cm. London, National Gallery

21. Leonardo da Vinci (1452–1519): '*The Virgin of the Rocks*.' About 1480. Panel transferred to canvas, 197 × 119·5 cm. Paris, Louvre

FORT WORTH PUBLIC LIBRARY

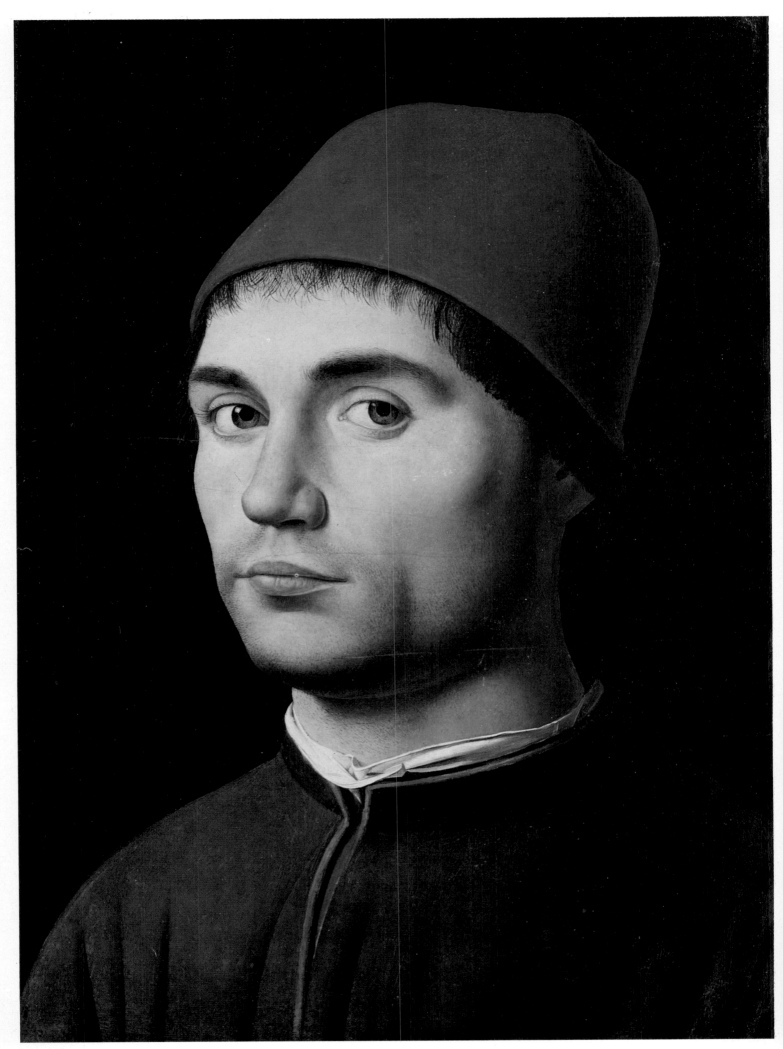

22. Antonello da Messina (active 1456; d. 1479): *Portrait of a Man*. About 1475. Panel, 35·6 × 25·5 cm.
London, National Gallery

23. Botticelli (*c*.1445–1510): *Portrait of a Young Man*. About 1480. Panel, 37·5 × 28·3 cm. London, National Gallery

24. Andrea del Castagno (c.1420–57): *The Young David*. About 1450. Leather, 115·6 × 76·9 × 41 cm. Washington, National Gallery of Art (Widener Collection)

25. Botticelli: *Venus*. Detail of Plate 26

26. Botticelli (c. 1445–1510): *The Birth of Venus*. About 1490. Canvas, 175 × 278 cm. Florence, Uffizi

FORT WORTH PUBLIC LIBRARY

27. Ascribed to Giorgione (*c.*1478–1510), but perhaps finished by Titian: *Fête Champêtre*. About 1510. Canvas, 110 × 138 cm. Paris, Louvre

28. Giovanni Bellini (active *c.*1459; d.1516): *The Doge Leonardo Loredan*. About 1501–5.
Panel, 61·5 × 45 cm. London, National Gallery

29. Leonardo da Vinci (1452–1519): *Portrait of a an Unknown Woman ('Mona Lisa')*. About 1506–8.
Panel, 76·8 × 53 cm. Paris, Louvre

30. Giovanni Bellini (active *c.*1459; d.1516): *The Feast of the Gods*. 1514. Canvas, 170 × 188 cm. Washington,

31. Raphael (1483–1520): 'The School of Athens.' About 1509–11. Fresco. Vatican, Stanza della Segnatura.

FORT WORTH PUBLIC LIBRARY

33. Michelangelo (1475–1564): *The Holy Family ('The Doni Tondo')*. About 1504. Panel, diameter 120 cm. Florence, Uffizi

32. Raphael (1483–1520): *The Virgin and Child with St. John the Baptist and St. Nicholas of Bari ('The Ansidei Madonna')*. 1505? Panel, 209·6 × 148·6 cm. London, National Gallery

34. Ascribed to Giorgione (*c.*1478–1510) : *The Virgin and Child with St. Anthony of Padua and St. Roch.* About 1508. Canvas, 92 × 133 cm. Madrid, Prado

35. Lorenzo Lotto (*c*.1480–1556) : *Portrait of Andrea Odoni*. 1527. Canvas, 101·5 × 114 cm. Hampton Court, Royal Collection (reproduced by gracious permission of Her Majesty the Queen)

36. Michelangelo (1475–1564): *The Creation of Adam*. 1511–12. Ceiling fresco. Vatican, Sistine Chapel

37. Pontormo (1494–1557): *Joseph in Egypt*. About 1515. Panel, 96·5 × 109·5 cm. London, National Gallery

38. Parmigianino (1503–40): *The Mystic Marriage of St. Catherine*. About 1530. Panel, 74·2 × 57 cm. London, National Gallery

39. Correggio (active 1514; d. 1534):
Jupiter and Io. About 1530. Canvas,
163·5 × 74 cm. Vienna,
Kunsthistorisches Museum

40. Rosso Fiorentino (1494–1540): *Moses and the Daughters of Jethro*. About 1520. Canvas, 160 × 117 cm. Florence, Uffizi

41. Bronzino (1503–72): *An Allegory*. About 1545/6. Panel, 146 × 116 cm. London, National Gallery

42. Domenico Puligo (1492–1527): *Portrait of a Young Nobleman*. About 1520–5. Panel,
114·2 × 83·5 cm. England, Private Collection

43. Giovanni Battista Moroni (active 1546–7; d. 1578): *Portrait of a Man ('The Tailor')*. About 1570. Canvas, 97·8 × 74·9 cm. London, National Gallery

44. Titian (*c*.1485/90–1576): *Pope Paul III and his Grandsons*. 1546. Canvas, 200 × 173 cm. Naples, Galleria Nazionale di Capodimonte

45. Jacopo Tintoretto (1518–94): *St. George and the Dragon*. About 1560–70.
Canvas, 157·5 × 100·3 cm. London, National Gallery

FORT WORTH PUBLIC LIBRARY

46. Jacopo Tintoretto (1518–94): *Susanna and the Elders*. About 1570. Canvas, 146·6 × 193·6 cm. Vienna, Kunsthistorisches Museum

47. Titian (*c.*1485/90–1576) : *Diana and her Nymphs surprised by Actaeon.* About 1556–9. Canvas, 188 × 203 cm. Edinburgh, National Gallery of Scotland (on loan from the Duke of Sutherland)

48. Paolo Veronese (1528?–88): *Mars and Venus united by Love*. About 1570–80. Canvas, 205·7 × 161 cm.
New York, Metropolitan Museum of Art (Kennedy Fund, 1910)

Janis Campbell & Cathy Collison

Janis Campbell and Cathy Collison have been friends and writing partners for 10 years. They are interested in sharing information with young people on every topic under the sun, from stars in the news to the stars in the sky. They met at the *Detroit Free Press*, where they write and edit for "Yak's Corner," a magazine-style section for young readers.

Janis has interviewed astronaut Dr. Mae Jemison. A dozen years ago, Cathy found herself answering many questions about space in a *Detroit Free Press* column, "News for Young Readers." More recently, she visited NASA's Kennedy Space Center for a story on the return to flight.

They have collaborated on several books, including *Authors by Request*, a book profiling 12 hot authors for young readers. Both live in Michigan and are married, with two children each. This is their first book with Sleeping Bear Press.

Alan Stacy

Alan created his first painting at the age of 18 months—on a wall at home! Luckily, his mother—also an artist—encouraged him from the start, enrolling him in an adult drawing class at the age of eight. Alan's father, an Air Force pilot, took the family to Germany, Virginia, Alaska, and New Mexico before settling in Texas in 1975. Alan credits his family's travels for his profound love of animals and nature, which is reflected in his art.

Alan worked in broadcast television as a graphic artist for many years before becoming a self-employed illustrator and designer. Alan also teaches cartooning, comic book art, and illustration. He is also the illustrator for *L is for Lone Star: A Texas Alphabet* and *Round Up: A Texas Number Book*. He lives in Arlington, Texas.

Alan's dad was part of the team that chose the astronauts for the *Gemini* and early *Apollo* space programs in the early 1960s.

Answers

1. Mercury
2. Neil Armstrong
3. At least two-thirds of the Earth is covered with water.
4. My Very Educated Mother Just Served Us Nine Pizzas.
5. Planet Pluto
6. Neptune

7. Sedna
8. Edmund Halley
9. Sally Ride
10. Uranus
11. Mars
12. Earth

End Notes:

Fred Whipple, a Harvard University astronomer, is credited with creating the term "dirty snowball" for a comet's nucleus.

* Astronomer Dr. Mike Brown of the California Institute of Technology in Pasadena, California, is the leader of the team that discovered Sedna.

An Out of This World Quiz

1. Which planet is closest to the sun?

2. Which astronaut was the first American to step foot on the moon?

3. Most of the Earth's surface is covered with what?

4. What sentence is a good one to help you remember the order and names of the planets?

5. What planet's name was suggested by an 11-year-old girl?

6. What is the name of the Roman god of the sea and a blue-looking planet?

7. What is the name of the new planetoid?

8. This astronomer predicted a comet would return. What is his name?

9. Who was the first American woman in space?

10. Which planet appears to be tilted on its side?

11. What planet is called the Red Planet?

12. What planet is not named after one of the gods or goddesses?

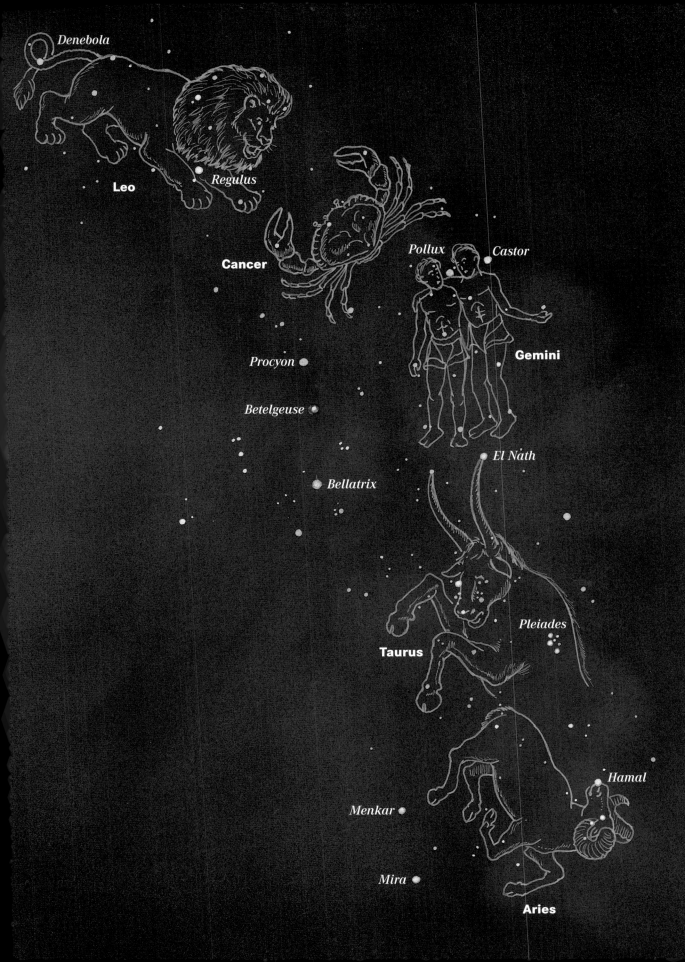

What's your sign? That's something people ask when they're talking about your zodiac sign. It all goes back to the Greeks, who saw animal patterns in the stars. They called the band of constellations the zodiac, or circle of animal signs. People used zodiac signs to tell fortunes and it is very popular. There's not any evidence that the stars affect your future, but many people enjoy reading horoscopes and keeping track of birth signs, or the constellations that were in the sky when you were born. Check your sign in the list below. Here are the dates that most horoscope watchers follow for identifying birthday signs.

Aries (*the ram*) March 21–April 19
Taurus (*the bull*) April 20–May 20
Gemini (*the twins*) May 21–June 20
Cancer (*the crab*) June 21–July 22
Leo (*the lion*) July 23–August 22
Virgo (*the virgin*) August 23–September 22
Libra (*the scales*) September 23–October 22
Scorpio (*the scorpion*) October 23–November 21
Sagittarius (*the archer*) November 22–December 21
Capricorn (*the goat*) December 22–January 19
Aquarius (*the water bearer*) January 20–February 18
Pisces (*the fish*) February 19–March 20

Sagittarius

Libra

Dschubba

Antares

Shaula

Scorpio

Virgo *Spica*

Capricorn

Aquarius

Skat

• *Fomalhaut*

Algenib

Pisces

Z is for Zodiac—
a name for 12 constellations.
The signs of the stars
have fascinated generations.

Y is for Year—
the time it takes to go 'round the sun.
For every planet,
the measure is a different one.

Each year, you have a birthday and it takes a long time until you celebrate again. But if you lived on Jupiter, it would take 12 times as long to reach that birthday. A Jupiter year is equal to 12 Earth years. A year is the time it takes for a planet to orbit around the sun. Like birthday parties? Then you would like Mercury, where a year is only about 88 days.

Here's how the other planets measure up in Earth-years.

Mercury: 88 Earth days
Venus: 225 Earth days
Earth: 365 days
Mars: 687 days
Jupiter: 4,333 days (12 Earth years)
Saturn: 10,759 days (about 30 Earth years)
Uranus: 30,685 days (about 84 Earth years)
Neptune: 60,189 days (about 164 Earth years)
Pluto: 90,465 days (about 248 Earth years)

Have you ever heard of Planet X? It's not a real planet, but was the way astronomers talked about the existence of a possible ninth planet in the early 1900s before Pluto was discovered. Astronomer Percival Lowell was sure there was a ninth planet, Planet X, and spent a lot of time searching for this planet until his death in 1916. He never found one, but his apprentice Clyde Tombaugh did in 1930.

Once Pluto was found, astronomers talked about the possibility of a Planet X beyond Pluto. Scientists have found a planetoid—too small to be a planet, but like a little cousin of the planet family. The discovery of Sedna, about three-quarters the size of Pluto, made of ice and rock, was announced in 2004. Sedna is the most distant known object in our solar system, at one point in its orbit, traveling about 84 billion miles away from the sun. Wow! Sedna is the name of an Inuit Arctic goddess of the sea and the discoverers of Sedna thought that would be the perfect name for this icy little planetoid.

X

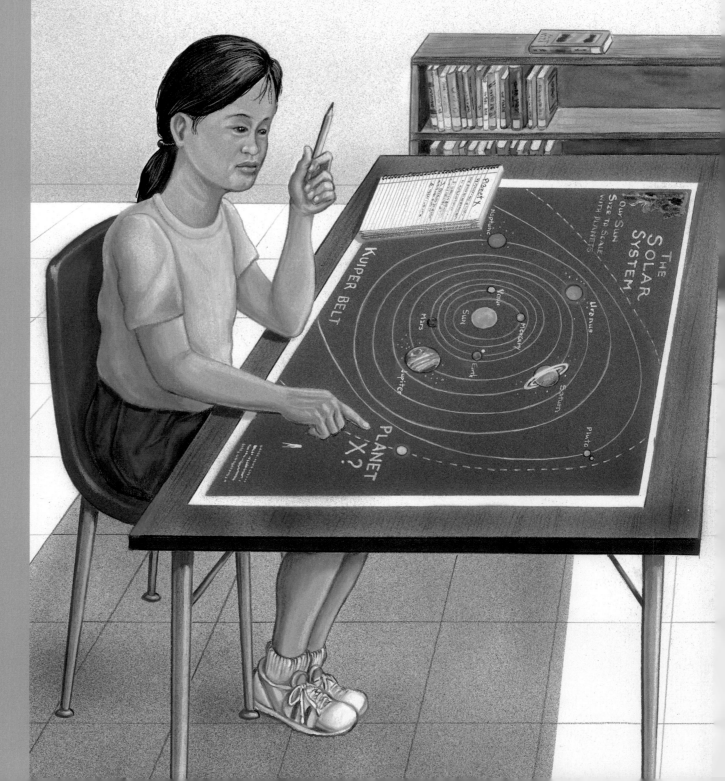

X is for Planet X,
    really just a name.
Finding another planet
    has been a tricky game.

W is for Wondering.
        Is there really life out there?
And W is for Water, too,
        which we hope to find somewhere.

W W

We know that water is the key to life. Without it, we couldn't exist. Two-thirds of the Earth is covered by water. On Mars, signs of frozen water on the planet's surface have been shown in different space probes. Space watchers are excited that signs of water may lead to signs of life on the Red Planet. Who knows what kind of life scientists could discover?

When did women get to space? In 1963, Valentina Tereshkova became the first woman in space when she orbited around the earth in the *Vostok 6* mission for the former Soviet Union. Twenty years later, the first American woman Sally Ride flew into space aboard space shuttle *Challenger*. In 1992, Dr. Mae Jemison became the first African-American woman to orbit in space on the space shuttle *Endeavour*.

V is for Venus,
a planet cloudy and hot,
with acid and poisonous gases,
it's quite an unlivable spot.

Venus is a bright beauty of a planet, but don't expect astronauts to visit.

Why? It's boiling hot; in fact it's hotter than boiling. Venus is hot enough that the surface is four times as hot as boiling water. Venus, named after the Roman goddess of love and beauty, wouldn't be livable for us. It is the second planet from the sun. The layer of thick clouds that adds to its beauty traps the heat in the planet so it can't escape. Scientists call this the greenhouse effect. You can see Venus at sunrise and sunset in certain times as the brightest star in the sky. Enjoy this planet from a distance.

U is for Uranus,
and for a Universe so unique,
where every star and planet
is one we want to seek.

You'll flip for Uranus, the planet on its side. Uranus is named after the Greek god of the sky. Uranus is the seventh planet away from the sun. As Uranus spins through the sky, it looks like a ball going through a hoop. Astronomers believe that a giant object at one time hit Uranus, tilting the planet on its side. Until Uranus was discovered in 1781 by William Herschel, people thought Saturn was on the edge of our solar system.

UFO stands for Unidentified Flying Object. Most scientists think that the UFOs can usually be explained as normal objects in space, including airplanes, comets, or shooting stars. Writers and moviemakers have had fun making UFOs come to life as alien spaceships.

U u

Thanks to the telescope, we are able to see the universe up close. Telescopes were used beginning in the early 1600s and changed the way we viewed the universe. A telescope makes objects appear brighter and clearer so we can see them better in the sky. There are many types of telescopes today that let scientists look at objects in space in different ways. Telescopes are powerful and important tools in the exploration of space.

Italian astronomer Galileo Galilei is believed to be the first to use a telescope to study the skies. He made many amazing discoveries. More recently, the powerful *Hubble* telescope orbiting around Earth sends back incredible pictures of planets, stars, and galaxies. The *Hubble* gets a visit about every three years from astronauts traveling on a space shuttle to repair anything that's broken. Hooray for the *Hubble*; it has opened up new windows on the worlds.

T is for the Telescope
that we use to watch the sky
to see if we can spot a star
or a comet flying by.

Tt

S

Ss

S is for Saturn
and for the sun, too.
And for the stars to wish upon
that make our dreams come true.

Saturn is a beauty. Saturn is the sixth planet away from the sun and the second biggest planet. Named for the Roman god of harvest time, it is famous for its beautiful rings that surround the planet. The rings are made of ice, rock, and dust. This is a very cold planet since it's so far from the sun.

The sun, an enormous hot star, is the center of our solar system. Our solar system is made up of the planets, and everything that orbits around the sun, from big Jupiter to tiny moons. The sun is made up of gases and although not the biggest star or brightest, it is the closest, at 93 million miles away from Earth. The sun is what makes our life on Earth thrive and survive.

Have you ever wished on a star and said the rhyme, "Star light, star bright, the first star I see tonight, I wish I may, I wish I might, have the wish I wish tonight." People have been saying that rhyme for hundreds of years. It goes back to the belief that wishing on stars is lucky and can make a wish come true.

R is for Robots
    that help us out in space.
R is also for the rovers
    that showed us Mars' red face.

Robots have been a huge help in exploring outer space. Robots can go where humans can't because they don't need to breathe, eat, or even sleep. The robot rovers on Mars are smart robots. In 2004 rovers named *Spirit* and *Opportunity* landed on Mars and began sending home amazing photos. NASA has big plans for robots in the future, especially to help us explore Mars. Robots will continue to be big helpers in future space exploration.

Rr

Q is for Quiet.
There's no sound in outer space.
You couldn't hear your friend talking,
even if you were face to face.

Quiet? How quiet? You can make as much noise as you want in outer space and it won't bother anyone. Sound can't travel when there's no air so it's completely quiet in outer space.

Q is also for questions. The sky has always fascinated us. Asking questions and watching the sky is something people have done for hundreds and hundreds of years. Sometimes asking questions can get people in trouble. Polish astronomer Nicolaus Copernicus questioned the idea more than 450 years ago that the Earth was the center of everything. He figured out that the sun must be the center of our solar system. Later astronomers proved him right. The more we learn about our stars and planets, the more questions we have. What's your question?

Saturn

Pluto

P is for Pluto—
a planet so small
that some people say
it's just like a little ice ball.

Pp

Pluto is the smallest planet in our solar system. Clyde Tombaugh discovered the planet in 1930 at Lowell Observatory in Flagstaff, Arizona. Pluto, Mickey Mouse's dog, was created by Walt Disney in honor of the new planet. Pluto is a pretty peculiar planet. It's very cold and at times becomes the eighth planet instead of the ninth planet from the sun when its orbit crosses inside the orbit of Neptune. The name of Pluto is for the Roman god of the underworld. An 11-year-old girl from Oxford, England, Venetia Burney, suggested the name Pluto.

This sentence is a good way to help remember the order and names of the planets:

My	Very	Educated	Mother	Just
E	E	A	A	U
R	N	R	R	P
C	U	T	S	I
U	S	H		T
R				E
Y				R

Served	Us	Nine	Pizzas
A	R	N	L
T	A	E	U
U	N	P	T
R	U	T	O
N	S	U	
		N	
		E	

Orbits are the paths the planets follow as they travel around the sun. An orbit is not like a highway with signs, but an invisible road. Don't worry, each planet knows its way. The sun's gravity keeps each planet on its right path. Look at this page to see how the nine planets follow their own paths.

O is for the Orbit
of planets 'round the sun.
Mercury's path is shortest.
Pluto has the longest one.

Mercury

Mars

Venus

Earth

Jupiter

Uranus

Neptune

N is for Neptune,
    a planet full of gas and ice.
If you had to live there,
    it wouldn't be so nice.

Neptune is named after the Roman god of the sea. Today, Neptune's icy-blue color reminds us of the sea. Neptune is the smallest of the family of gassy planets. There are four of them—Neptune, Jupiter, Saturn, and Uranus. Neptune is never likely to be a place astronauts will visit. Clouds of poisonous gases surround the planet. It's a frozen, cold place about 2.8 billion miles from the sun. Neptune wasn't discovered until 1846.

NASA is the name of the National Aeronautics and Space Administration—the people in charge of the United States program to explore space. In 1958 the group was formed by the U.S. government and got started working on the possibility of sending humans to explore space. The rest is history! NASA is now focusing on finishing work on the International Space Station and Mars exploration.

M is for Mercury,
    closest to the sun.
And for Mars,
    the only red one.

Mercury is the closet planet to the sun, but it's still about 36 million miles away from the sun. It's small and swift—one year on Mercury —the time it takes the planet to orbit around the sun—is only 88 days on Earth. The zippy little planet is named after the winged messenger god, Mercury, of the Romans. On Mercury, the temperatures are boiling hot in the daytime, about 800 degrees Fahrenheit. But the weather report for nights on Mercury is always the same: freezing cold, about—350 degrees Fahrenheit.

Mars is named after another Roman god, the god of war. It's also nicknamed the Red Planet, because of its color. We are learning more about the rocky red planet everyday as robots explore the land. It's more like Earth than other planets. It's the fourth planet from the sun and about half the size of Earth. A Martian day would be only half an hour longer than an Earth day. Could you live there? No, at least not right now. The air is too thin and the planet is too cold. But recent signs that Mars once had water has everyone excited to learn more about mysterious Mars.

M
m

is for looking up. The night sky is a
show that is always changing. One of the
ways to keep track of the stars is by finding pictures or constellations in the
nighttime sky. Shapes in the stars—like a
big pan called the Big Dipper—are easy to
spot once you know how. It's just like a
dot-to-dot picture in your coloring book.

is for light, too. Stargazers will tell you
that city lights can give off such a glow
that it can spoil the sky show. For better
viewing, it's often best to head with your
family to the country, or to a beach or
park, where you're not in the middle of
the streetlights. Vacation is a good time
to look at stars.

is also for Leo the Lion, a favorite picture
to spot in the stars. For help on finding Leo
and other star pictures, head to a local
planetarium. A planetarium is a domed the-
ater that projects lights to form the stars
and planets and shows their movements
in the sky. A planetarium show will illustrate what you can see on the big sky
screen in the night sky.

Check with local astronomy clubs, who
sometimes organize star-watching parties.

L¹

L is for Looking up
to explore the amazing skies.
Astronomers give us charts and maps
to follow planets with our eyes.

Hercules

Corona
Borealis

Boötes

Alphecca

Arcturus

STAR CHART

K is for Kennedy,
the president with a plan
for us to race to outer space
and find out all we can.

K k

President John F. Kennedy is the leader given credit for pushing the United States forward in space exploration. When he became president, there was a race for exploring outer space. Russian cosmonaut Yury Gagarin was the first person in space and first person to orbit the Earth. President Kennedy wanted the United States to be the first country to put a man on the moon. That goal was accomplished in July of 1969 when Neil Armstrong set foot on the moon. Today you can visit the Kennedy Space Center by Cape Canaveral, Florida. The center is named in honor of President Kennedy.

In 2004, President George W. Bush announced big new goals for America's space program, including building a new spacecraft that could take astronauts to the space station and beyond. Maybe there will even be a return trip to the moon, making the moon a station to launch more missions.

Jupiter is the giant of our galaxy. This huge planet is the largest in our solar system. Giant Jupiter is 300 times heavier than Earth. Jupiter has great gravity so the temperatures are high. But around the planet are stormy clouds of poisonous gases, and it's freezing cold. This king-sized planet is named after the king of the Roman gods. Jupiter is also known by its storms and something called the Great Red Spot. The spot doesn't stay in one place, but is actually a big gas storm, swirling around the planet.

The illustration shows the four largest of the many moons of Jupiter.

Io

Europa

Ganymede

Callisto

J is for Jupiter—
the biggest planet of them all,
where it is always cold and stormy,
and there is no spring or fall.

Jj

I is for the International Space Station. It is truly international with 16 countries helping to build and operate this laboratory in space. The space station has been up in orbit since 1998. The first crew arrived in 2000. The station is a place where space scientists can do experiments while continuing to work on building the giant space structure. The space station should be finished by 2010.

Imagine you might someday travel to outer space. What would you wear? What would you want to do there? Plenty of writers and moviemakers have used their imagination to show us a far-out vision of space. Moviemaker George Lucas imagined an amazing world in his *Star Wars* movies. *E.T.* was Steven Spielberg's movie using his imagination on what would happen if a friendly alien came to Earth. Let your imagination take off!

I is for International.
    Because studying space is a global quest,
on the International Space Station
    we have crews from East and West.

H h

H is for Halley.
Hip, hip hooray!
He predicted a comet's return
so it's named after him today.

Astronomer Edmund Halley isn't the only one who thinks comets are cool. The comet is an icy ball revolving around the sun—with a tail of dust and gas. Comet followers call them dirty snowballs ever since an astronomer used that description in 1950. Or you could say a comet looks like a star with long, flowing hair trailing behind it. The Greeks saw comets like that and called them *aster kometes*, or hairy stars. People used to think these comets came at any time and sometimes were afraid of them, thinking the comet was a sign of some bad news.

Edmund Halley changed that thinking. The English astronomer was the first person to recognize that comets had an orbit too. Halley was so good at studying comets, he was able to predict when one comet would return. That comet is named after him. Halley's comet returns about every 76 years. It was last seen flying by in 1986 and will come again in about 2061. Does that sound like a long time? It is, but don't worry, there will be other comets you can catch flying by.

Library Media C

G is for Galaxy,
a big family of stars so bright.
Ours is called the Milky Way,
a small part we see each night.

Gg

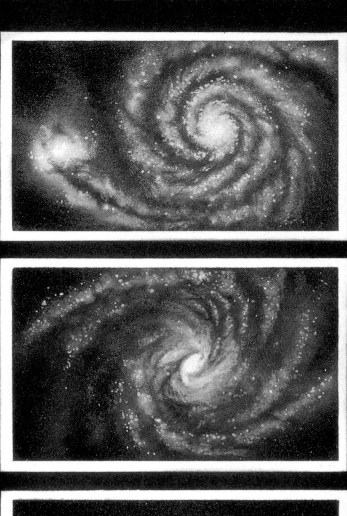

A galaxy is a family of stars, but in such a huge family you'd never meet every member. There are billions of stars in one galaxy. Planets are part of a galaxy, too. So are dust and gases. Gravity keeps the family together. We are in the Milky Way galaxy. It is a huge galaxy of about 100 billion stars, but astronomers remind us that the Milky Way is just one galaxy out of billions. Galaxies come in different shapes and sizes. Our galaxy has been compared to a big pinwheel.

F is for Footprints
   astronauts left on the moon.
Because there's no wind or rain,
   they won't go away anytime soon.

Footprints in the sand or the snow on Earth don't last very long. But did you know there are footprints on the moon that will last for thousands of years? The footprints are from the astronauts who have walked on the moon. On July 20, 1969, American astronaut Neil Armstrong made the first human footprint on the moon. Neil's words are still famous. He said, "That's one small step for man, one giant leap for mankind." Besides footprints, Neil and astronaut Buzz Aldrin left an American flag and a plaque on the moon. Also on that famous mission, called *Apollo 11*, was astronaut Michael Collins. The message on the plaque says, "We came in peace for all mankind."

Ff

E is for Earth.
Our planet's so much fun.
Luckily for us, we're the right
distance from the sun.

Home, sweet home. The Earth is our home and it sure is one sweet planet. In fact, Earth is the only place in our galaxy that we know of that can support human life. All of the planets except Earth are named after gods or goddesses. The name Earth comes from an old English word, meaning base or ground. Earth is the third planet from the sun. We have the right atmosphere for life with plenty of oxygen and plenty of water. The Earth orbits at a tilt like a spinning top. Each day is 24 hours long and it takes about 365 days for the Earth to orbit the sun.

E is also for Earth Day. Our environment is special, and people want to make sure we keep treating it with care. So every year we celebrate and look for new ways to take care of our planet on April 22.

The disappearance of the dinosaurs is a bit of a mystery. What caused this to happen? One idea is that a huge meteorite hit the Earth. Many scientists believe that a comet or asteroid hit our planet 65 million years ago with so much force that it was like a gigantic bomb exploding, causing huge destruction. It may have set off earthquakes, tidal waves, and caused big clouds of dust and debris. These dusty clouds may have blocked the sun and brought darkness and cold for months on end. That drastic change in the climate meant the dinosaurs could not survive, although other living creatures could.

D is also for dogs in space. Two dogs survived a trip to outer space in 1960 when Belka and Strelka orbited the Earth in the Soviet Union's spacecraft. Later, President Kennedy was given a puppy of Strelka's as a gift.

Dd

D is the Dinosaurs,
the giant creatures who made Earth home.
But when a mighty comet struck,
they would no longer roam.

C c
C
C

C is for Crater,
deep and sometimes round.
The huge hole is a sure sign
that a meteorite once hit the ground.

On Earth you can find craters, large holes left when a meteoroid, or large rock from space, smashes down into the Earth. If this meteoroid doesn't burn up before hitting the ground, then it's called a meteorite. Other planets and moons also have craters. One of the best-known craters in the United States is near Winslow, Arizona. The word crater comes from the Greek language. The Greek word, *krater*, means bowl.

Big bang! Is that a noise? No, big bang is the name of a big idea—a theory that explains how the universe began. Many scientists believe that the universe began with a huge explosion about 13 billion or more years ago. This explosion, or bang, led to the creation of the building blocks of the universe, which began forming our galaxies. Even though this happened billions of years ago, astronomers think the effect is still happening today as our universe continues to grow.

B is also for black holes. Imagine a big black invisible space, like a dark hole. That's what scientists believe happens when a large star explodes or dies, leaving a huge amount of gravity. Black holes sound mysterious and they are. Scientists hope to find out more about them.

B is for the Big Bang;
no, not a crashing sound,
but the beginning of the universe,
according to what scientists have found.

A is for Astronomy,
　　　the science of outer space.
　It's how we explore the nighttime sky,
　　　and keep track of each planet's place.

Astronomy is the study of space—including the stars, planets, and galaxies. It's a science both old and new. Even today, astronomers are always making new discoveries. Maybe you'll want to be one, too.

A is for astronauts. Think of them as sailors in space. The word comes from the Greek language. *Astron* means star and *nautes* means sailor. America's astronaut program got its start in the late 1950s and early '60s. Alan B. Shepard became the first American in space on May 5, 1961, shortly after a Russian cosmonaut (the word the Russians use for astronaut) had orbited the Earth on April 12, 1961. John Glenn became the first American to orbit the Earth on February 20, 1962.

A is also for asteroids. They are giant rocks in space, almost acting like very tiny planets. They orbit the sun in a path, which runs mainly between Mars and Jupiter.

Aa
A

For Andrew, Colin, and Steve—
the brightest stars in my universe.

JANIS

For Dad, who always taught me to shine.
And for my other stars: Bill, Maggie, and Robert.

CATHY

For Dad, who had his part in making the dream of space
exploration a reality; for both of my parents, who gave me a sense
of imagination and a wonder about life and all creation.

Deo gratia

ALAN

A special thank you to the super stars at Michigan State University's
Abrams Planetarium—David Batch, Shane Horvatin, and John French
—for being our first readers and giving us great advice.

—*Janis and Cathy*

Text Copyright © 2005 Janis Campbell and Cathy Collison
Illustration Copyright © 2005 Alan Stacy

All rights reserved. No part of this book may be reproduced in any manner
without the express written consent of the publisher, except in the case of brief
excerpts in critical reviews and articles. All inquiries should be addressed to:

Sleeping Bear Press

310 North Main Street, Suite 300
Chelsea, MI 48118
www.sleepingbearpress.com

© 2005 Thomson Gale, a part of the Thomson Corporation.

Thomson, Star Logo and Sleeping Bear Press are trademarks
and Gale is a registered trademark used herein under license.

Printed and bound in Canada.

10 9 8 7 6 5 4 3 2

Library of Congress Cataloging-in-Publication Data

Collison, Catherine.
G is for galaxy : an out of this world alphabet / by Cathy Collison and Janis
Campbell ; illustrated by Alan Stacy.
p. cm.
Summary: "This A to Z children's pictorial covers topics such as the planets,
craters, comets, orbits, and telescopes. Each word related to our galaxy or to space
is introduced with a simple poem for younger readers and also includes detailed
expository text for older readers"—Provided by publisher.
ISBN 1-58536-255-7
1. Astronomy—Dictionaries, Juvenile. 2. Astronomy—Pictorial works—
Juvenile literature. I. Campbell, Janis (Janis M.) II. Stacy, Alan, ill. III. Title.
QB46.C743 2005
520'.3—dc22   2005006023

G is for Galaxy

An Out of This World Alphabet

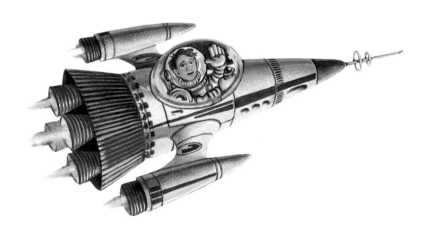

Library Media Center
McCarty School
3000 Village Green Drive
Aurora, IL 60504
630-375-3407

300200092483X

Written by Janis Campbell & Cathy Collison and Illustrated by Alan Stacy

W9-AYZ-955